Unit 1

Nationalities

Fill in the nationalities.

1. Zlatko comes from Dubrovnik. He's ... *Yugoslavian* ...
2. Janet is from Bristol. She's ....
3. Alec lives in Toronto. He's ....
4. Mr Carpenter comes from Edinburgh. He's ....
5. Mario lives in Naples. He's ....
6. Greta comes from Bonn. She's ....
7. Pat is from Melbourne. She's ....

Now try these nationalities.

1. George Washington was ....
2. Pele is ....
3. General de Gaulle was ....
4. Aristotle Onassis was ....
5. Michelangelo was ....
6. Paul McCartney is ....

Work

Zlatko is a student. (*Regency School of English; 3 weeks*)

Zlatko studies at the Regency School of English. He's studied there for 3 weeks.

Now write about these people in the same way.

1. Mary is a secretary. (*office; 2 years*)

   ....

2. George is an English teacher. (*Regency School of English; 18 months*)

   ....

3. James is a businessman. (*office; 20 years*)

   ....

4. I'm ....

   ....

Unit 1

Places

Jenny/hostel/city/SE Britain

1. *Jenny lives in a hostel in a city in the south east of Britain*

    Now write about these other people in the same way.

2. David/flat/large town/near sea/NW Britain

    ....

3. Mary/cottage/country/SW Germany

    ....

4. Harry/house/small town/S Italy

    ....

Linking sentences

Link the right sentences together, using so.

I haven't got any money		I don't know London.
I've lived in England		I don't know many words.
I've only studied English for a month	so	I want to find a job.
I've never been to England		I speak English quite well.

1. ....
2. ....
3. ....
4. ....

Now link them using because.

1. *I want to find a job because I haven't got any money.*
2. ....
3. ....
4. ....

Whose is it?

Office (her – not me) ... *That's her office. It isn't mine.*

Now write about the things below.

1. Book (not you – him) ....

2. Paper (me – not you) ....

Unit 1

3. Desk (Rod – not me) ....
4. Ticket (not Jenny – Rod) ....
5. Phone (secretary – not Rod) ....

Talking about people

Read this description of a musician on a record cover:

This is Steve. He's American and he comes from New York. He lives in a flat in a London suburb. Steve plays the guitar, and he sings, too. He's been in the band for two years. He likes dancing and playing chess in his spare time.

Now write descriptions of the other three people in the band.

Manchester
cottage/country
piano/guitar
6 months
gardening/running

This is Kevin. ....
....
....
....

Detroit
house/London
drums/sings
a year
going to discos /
reading

This is Ed. ....
....
....
....

Paris
house/village
near London
sings/flute
2 years
listening to
music/dancing

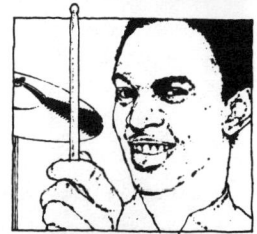

This is Marianne. ....
....
....
....

Unit 2

Likes and dislikes

Look at the information below, and then write a paragraph about each person.

		👍	👎	🤷
	Jane's a nurse. She has to	work in a hospital look after people	give injections work at weekends	work at night wear a uniform
	Neil's a policeman. He has to	drive a police car wear a uniform	control football crowds arrest people	do shiftwork work at night
	Mary's an air stewardess. She has to	travel abroad stay in hotels	fly in bad weather help rude passengers	help polite passengers serve meals
	Fred's a technician. He has to	work in a factory mend machines	do shiftwork train assistants	work on his own clean machines

1. JANE: I'm a nurse. I like working in a hospital and ....
   ...., but I don't like giving injections or ....
   On the other hand, I don't mind working at night or ....

2. NEIL: I'm a policeman. I like ...., but ....
   .... or .... On the other hand, ...
   .... or ....

3. MARY: I'm ....
   ....
   ....

4. FRED: ....
   ....
   ....

Talking about other people's likes and dislikes

Write five sentences about Harold like this:

People smoke while Harold is eating, but he doesn't mind.

Harold doesn't mind people smoking while he's eating.

_____ Unit 2

1. Harold's son borrows his car, but he doesn't mind.

   Harold ....

2. His daughter stays out late, and he doesn't like it.

   ....

3. People laugh at his jokes, and he likes it.

   ....

4. His wife talks while he's watching TV, but he doesn't mind.

   ....

5. People use his telephone without asking, and he doesn't like it.

   ....

Giving opinions

Match the sentences in column A with the adjectives in column B.

A		B
1. She never says hello. 2. He never stops talking. 3. She still likes the Beatles. 4. That house has too many people in it. 5. I'd like a coat like that. 6. I don't like that building 7. That book's all about death. 8. I like studying philosophy.	I think he's she's it's	a. ugly. b. overcrowded. c. unfriendly. d. depressing. e. fascinating. f. boring. g. old fashioned. h. lovely.

Write your answers here:

1 ...., 2 ...., 3 ...., 4 ...., 5 ...., 6 ...., 7 ...., 8 ....

Now give your opinions about different things, using the adjectives provided.

1. I think ... *pink trouser-suits are* .... ugly.

2. I think .... marvellous.

3. I think .... dull.

4. .... interesting.

5. .... beautiful.

6. .... friendly.

Making suggestions

Reply to these remarks with a suggestion, using What about, How about **or** Why don't we, **like this:**

We're not getting enough exercise.

Why don't we go out for a run?

Unit 2

1. We're not getting enough exercise.

   ....

2. I've got a holiday on Monday.

   ....

3. We ought to take Aunt Emily out somewhere.

   ....

4. There's nothing good on the TV tonight.

   ....

5. I'm forgetting all my French.

   ....

Now reply to each of your suggestions, and make another, using Let's **or** I'd rather, **like this:**

I'm not so keen on running. Let's go out for a walk instead.

1. *I'm not so keen on* .... *Let's* ....
2. ....
3. ....
4. ....
5. ....

Comprehension

Read this letter, and then answer the questions.

> 11 Gloucester Terrace,
> Torquay,
> Devon
> 8th August
>
> Dear Wendy,
> I haven't heard from you for months. Do write and tell me how you are. I'm working at a guest house for the summer, so life's pretty busy. I like meeting all the guests, and helping in the dining room, though I'm not keen on making the beds and cleaning all the bathrooms!
> I have to sit on reception, too, sometimes, but I don't mind doing that — there's always something interesting going on.
> One of the guests is an Italian called Luigi. I think he's marvellous. He's tall and attractive, and he's a bit old-fashioned. Whenever he sees me he kisses my hand! He's very friendly, and he talks to me a lot. He loves water-skiing, and he's keen on walking, too. I'm going to take him for a long walk in the country on my day off. He doesn't like the beach here, because he says it's too crowded.
> I've just had a great idea. Why don't you come down here from London for the weekend? You can meet lots of interesting people at the guest house. I know you'll like them. We can go swimming and go for long walks too — the countryside's beautiful around here.
> See you soon,
> Love
> Janet

_____ Unit 2

1. Where is Janet working for the summer? ....
2. What jobs does she like doing? ....
3. What jobs doesn't she like doing? ....
4. What job doesn't she mind doing? ....
   Why?...
5. Who is Luigi? ....
6. Write down five adjectives which describe what Luigi is like.
   (i) .... (ii) .... (iii) .... (iv) .... (v) ....
7. What does Luigi like doing? ....
8. Why doesn't Luigi like the beaches in Torquay? ....
9. What does Janet suggest to Wendy? She suggests that she ....
   ....
10. What three things can Wendy do if she comes to Torquay?
    (i) .... (ii) .... (iii) ....

Vocabulary

Write three adjectives describing each of the following:

1. your capital city (i)............(ii)............(iii)............ 2. television (i)............
   (ii)............(iii)............ 3. modern fashion (i)............(ii)............(iii)............

Unit 3

Talking about health

Write the missing words in the crossword.

Clues

(A = Across; D = Down)

A. JILL: Hello, Mum. How are you today?

   MRS GREY: I don't feel .... (16A) well, I'm afraid.

   JILL: Oh, ... (10A). ...... (13A) sorry.
             What's the ......? (14D)

   MRS GREY: I've ...... (1A) an awful ...... (7A) in my shoulder.

   JILL: Why don't you ...... (2D) some medicine?

Unit 3

MRS GREY: The doctor ...... (11D) me some medicine last night, but it didn't help.

JILL: What about your back?

MRS GREY: That's ...... (19A) ...... (22A) today.

JILL: Oh good. I am ...... (11A). Well, I must go. George ...... (5D) his love. And here's today's newspaper for you to ...... (17D).

MRS GREY: ...... (3A), dear. Goodbye.

JILL: Bye. I'll come and see you ...... (15A) tomorrow.

B. LIL: How's your headache?

ANN: Not too ...... (1D), I'm afraid.

LIL: Why don't you ...... (2D) an ...... (4D)?

ANN: Yes, I will. I think I've got a ...... (3D), too. I feel very ...... (20D). I think I'll spend the ...... (12D) in bed.

C. FRED: What's the ...... (14D)? You look ...... (9D).

DAVE: I am. I've got a stomach ...... (6A).

FRED: Perhaps you ...... (18A) too ...... (19A) for dinner last night.

DAVE: Yes, I think I ...... (21A).

FRED: You always eat too ...... (19A). Why don't you ...... (17D) the diet questionnaire in Building Strategies, Unit 3? Then you can check your ...... (8A)!

Asking about the past

Mrs Smith is answering questions about her morning. You write the questions.

1. Did .... ?

   Yes, I did. I got up at 6.00.

2. Did .... ?

   No, I didn't. I only had a cup of coffee.

3. What time .... ?

   I left the house at 8.00.

4. Where .... ?

   I went to the shops.

5. What .... ?

   I bought food for the whole family.

6. Did ....

   No I didn't. The bus didn't come, so I had to walk.

Routines

Read this passage, then write on page 9 about Sandra Rogers' routine. Imagine you are Sandra Rogers.

Sandra Rogers had a typical day yesterday. She got up at 7.30 and gave the children their breakfast at 8.00. Then at 8.30 she took them to school and drove to the office. She had a light lunch at 1.00 and did some shopping. She left the office at 3.30 and picked her children up from school at 4.00. She gave them their supper at 5.00 and at 6.00 she started the housework.

Unit 3

7.30 ..... *I get up.* .....
8.00 .....
8.30 .....
1.00 .....
3.30 .....
4.00 .....
5.00 .....

Comprehension

Read this passage, and then answer the questions below.

Jim Clough got up at 7.00 this morning. He had a good breakfast, and then he left the house. Jim usually drives to work, but it was a nice morning, so he walked. He went through the park, and then he started to cross Church Street. Unfortunately, he didn't look very carefully, and while he was crossing the road a cyclist ran into him. Jim fell down and hurt his arm.

His wife gave him lunch in bed, and after lunch the doctor came. He looked at Jim's arm, and said, 'I'm sorry, Mr Clough, but I'm afraid you must stay in bed for three days.'

'Three days?' said Jim.

'Yes,' said the doctor. 'I'm sorry.'

But Jim looked happy. 'Sorry?' he said. 'I'm not, I'm glad. The big football match is on Friday. Now I can watch it at home on the TV!'

1. What time did Jim get up? .....
2. What did he do after breakfast? .....
3. How does Jim usually get to work? .....
4. Why did he walk this morning? .....
5. Where did the accident happen? .....
6. How did the accident happen? .....
7. What happened to Jim when the cyclist hit him? .....
8. Where did Jim have lunch? .....
9. What happened after lunch? .....
10. What does Jim have to do? .....

Writing about the past

**Read the story about Jim again, and look at Clare Robins' diary.
Then write on page 10 about Clare Robins' day.**

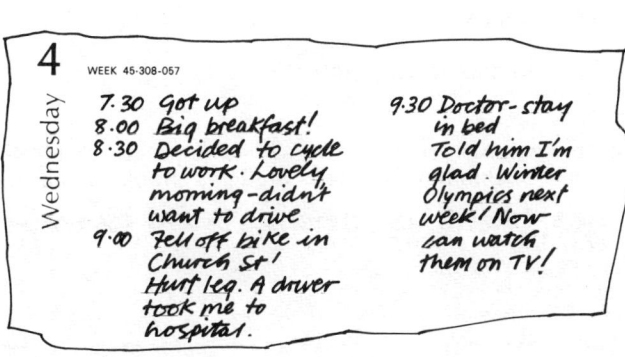

Unit 3

Clare Robins got up at 7.30. She .... Clare usually ...., but it was .... so .... At 9.00 she was in Church Street. Unfortunately, while she .... a man stepped out in front of her, and she ran into him. She .... A driver stopped and ...., ... The doctor .... and said '.. .' 'A week?' said Clare. 'Yes,' '.. .' But *Clare* .... 'Sorry?' she said. '..................................... !'

Unit 4

Facilities and directions

You are staying with a friend, Paul, in Portland. Ask questions about the facilities, like this:

1. I need some medicine. *Is there a good chemist near here?*
2. I'd like a swim. ....
3. How about a Chinese meal? ....
4. I haven't got any money. ....
5. I need a new jacket. ....
6. I want to send a telegram. ....
7. I haven't seen a film for a long time. ....
8. I need a hair cut. ....
9. Why don't we go dancing? ....
10. Let's go and have a drink. ....

You are Paul. Answer your friend's first five questions and tell him where the facilities are. (Use the map at the beginning of Unit 4 of Building Strategies Students' Book to help you.)

1. *Yes, there's a chemist in Elm St, opposite the supermarket.*
2. ....
3. ....

4. ....
5. ....

Now direct your friend to the same five places.

You are in the house opposite 'All About Flowers', in the *top left hand corner* of the map.

1. Go out of the house, cross the road and walk down Birch St as far as the traffic lights. Then turn left into Elm St, and the Chemist is about half way down, on the left.

2. ....
   ....

3. ....
   ....

4. ....
   ....

5. ....
   ....

Giving directions

A man stops Paul outside the ABC cinema in Poplar Street and asks him the way to the bus station. Write their conversation in the right order. (Use the map at the beginning of Unit 4 of Building Strategies Students' Book.)

MAN:	....	a. So I go down Elm Street, and turn left at the lights into Birch Street. And the bus station is there.
PAUL:	....	b. Ah, is that Birch Street?
MAN:	....	c. Yes, there is. It's in Birch Street.
PAUL:	....	d. The first turning on the right?
MAN:	....	e. Excuse me. Is there a bus station in Portland?
PAUL:	....	f. Yes, that's Birch Street. The bus station is about 500 metres down Birch Street, on the right.
MAN:	....	g. You're welcome.
PAUL:	....	h. How do I get there?
MAN:	....	i. Fine. Thanks very much.
PAUL:	....	j. Yes, that's right. You'll be in Elm Street. Go down Elm Street as far as the traffic lights. There's a supermarket on the corner. And then you turn left.
MAN:	....	k. Yes, that's right. You can't miss it. It's opposite the hospital.
PAUL:	....	l. Well, you go down the street and take the first turning on the right.

Unit 4

Comprehension

Read this newspaper column, and answer the questions.

Ron Cousin's Guide to Good Eating

The northern suburb of Sutton doesn't appear in this year's Good Food Guide. There are few facilities of any kind for the 19,000 people who live there, and people come into Bristol when they want to eat out. Until last Saturday I thought there weren't any restaurants in Sutton, apart from a few fish and chip shops, and one or two hamburger cafes.

So what happened last Saturday? A friend of mine took me out to dinner. We got off the bus at Sutton Central, and walked down George Road to the post office. Then we turned left into Market Street, and right into a little street called West Lane, between two blocks of flats.

The Rajah restaurant in West Lane only has six tables, and it was empty when we arrived, but we had a wonderful Indian meal there. The Tandoori chicken was very tasty, and the curries were hot and delicious. The wine was good and cheap, and the meal only cost £12 for two.

Try it – but hurry. You can't seat 19,000 people at only six tables!

1. Is it true that Ron Cousin
   a. likes Sutton? ......
   b. doesn't mind Sutton? ......
   c. doesn't like Sutton? ......

2. Where do people in Sutton usually go if they want to eat out?
   ....
   ....

3. What two sorts of eating places are there in Sutton apart from the Rajah restaurant?
   (i) ....
   ....
   (ii) ....
   ....

4. What happened last Saturday?
   ....
   ....

5. Give directions to the Rajah restaurant.
   (i) ....
   ....
   (ii) ....
   ....
   (iii) ....
   ....
   (iv) ....
   ....

6. Do a lot of people know about
   the Rajah restaurant?

   ....

7. How does Ron Cousin describe

   a. The Tandoori chicken? ....

   b. the curries? ....

   c. the wine? ....

8. Why must people hurry if they
   want to eat at the Rajah?

   ....

Except for and *As well as*

| Except for

As well as | a big supermarket
a disco
a football ground | there are | no good
plenty of
other | shopping facilities
entertainment facilities
sports facilities | in this town. |

1. **Write three sentences using** except for.

   a. ....

   b. ....

   c. ....

2. **Write three sentences using** as well as.

   a. ....

   b. ....

   c. ....

Vocabulary

Draw a map of your city, town or village and label it.

Unit 5

Linking ideas

Link the ideas in these sentences, using when.

1. He saw the room and he liked it.
   When ....

2. I asked for permission to use the phone, but he refused.
   ....

3. He woke up and fell out of bed.
   ....

4. I got home and made a cup of tea.
   ....

Asking and refusing permission

A: I'm hot. *Do you mind if I turn off the heating?*
B: *Sorry, but the house plants need to be in a warm room.*

Write more conversations like the one above. Use these expressions to ask for permission: Can I, May I, Do you mind if, Is it all right if, **and answers like:** Well actually **and** Sorry, but.

1. A: I haven't got any more cigarettes. ....
   B: *Sorry,* ....

2. A: I need to wash my hands. ....
   B: ....

3. A: I can't find a babysitter. ....
   B: ....

4. A: Oh dear. I haven't got any money. ....
   B: ....

5. A: Oh. The news is on in a few minutes. ....
   B: ....

6. A: I've missed the last bus home. ....
   B: ....

Unit 5

Furniture and fittings

Look at these twelve things:

armchair	fridge	bed	bath
dressing table	shower	sofa	cooker
washbasin	bookcase	sink	wardrobe

Which three would you find in:

a. a bedroom? (i) .... (ii) .... (iii) ....

b. a bathroom? (i) .... (ii) .... (iii) ....

c. a kitchen? (i) .... (ii) .... (iii) ....

d. a sitting room? (i) .... (ii) .... (iii) ....

Asking about houses

Mrs Smith is answering questions about her new house. You ask the questions.

1. *What shape is the sitting room?*

   The sitting room? It's L-shaped.

2. ....

   The kitchen? It's white.

3. ....

   The front door? It's made of wood and glass.

4. ....

   The garden? It's long and rectangular.

5. ....

   The bedroom wallpaper? It's green, with a flowery pattern.

Furniture for sale

You're selling these pieces of furniture. Write an advertisement describing them, to put in the post office window.

FOR SALE
Dark round wooden dining table £20
Tel: 318529

Now write sentences describing them.

1. *The dining table is dark and round, and is made of wood.*

2. ....

3. ....

4. ....

Unit 5

Comprehension

Read this description of a bed-sitting room, and draw in the furniture in the right places in the plan.

The room is L-shaped. There's a round dining table and four chairs opposite the kitchen door – I can look out into the garden when I have dinner. My record-player is in the corner, between the kitchen door and the small window. There are bookcases on both sides of the fireplace, and a rectangular coffee table in front of the fire. My bed is against the long wall, under the large window. I use it as a sofa during the day, so there are some big, striped cushions on it. Opposite the bed, against the kitchen wall, there's a desk, and between the bed and the desk there's a large armchair. I like sitting and reading in front of the fire with my feet up on the coffee table. In the empty space in front of the door, there's an oval carpet on the floor. And the piano's in the corner between the door and my bed.

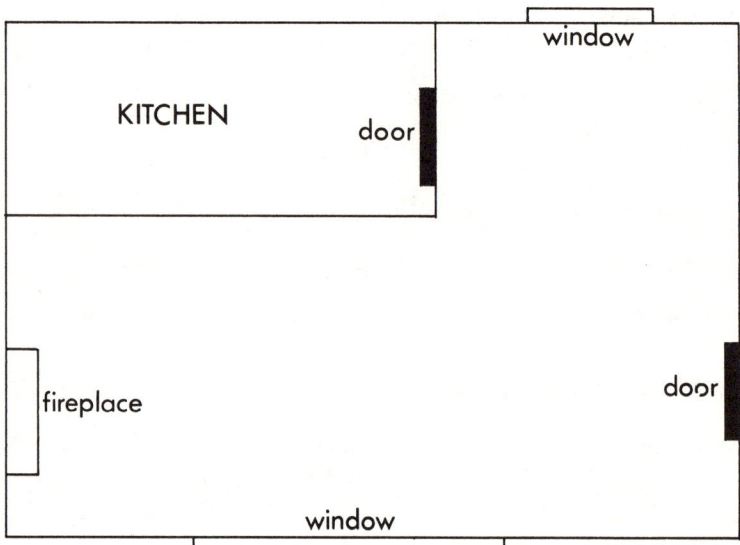

Describing a room

Now describe this room, and the furniture in it.

The room is r ....

....

....

....

....

....

....

....

....

....

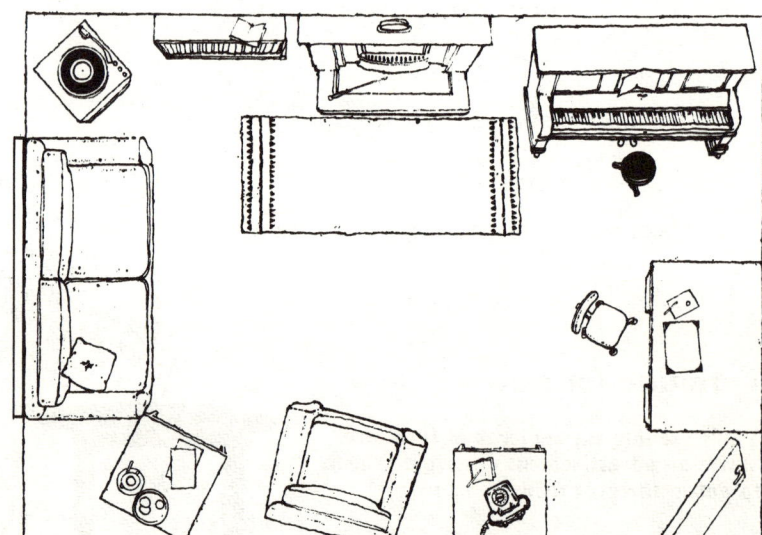

16

Unit 6

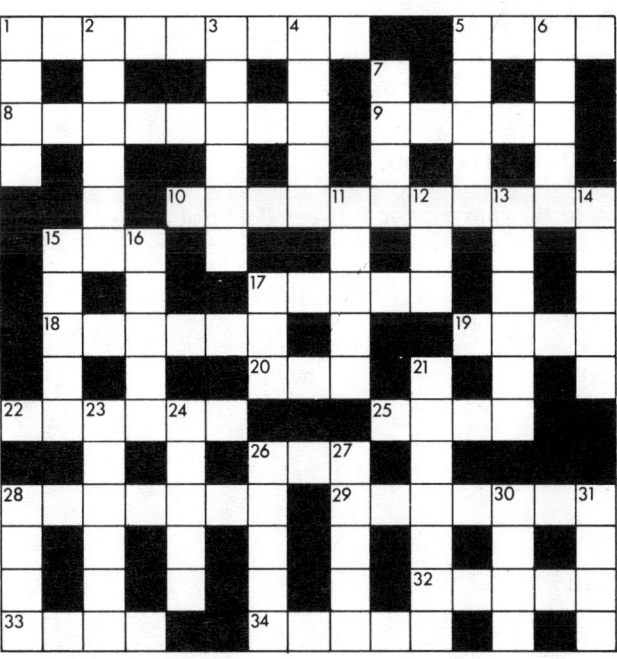

Crossword

Write the missing words in the crossword

Clues

Across

1. We didn't have an enjoyable time. We had a .... time! (9)
5. He's bored. He sees the .... people every day. (4)
8. Barbara is Mrs Cooper's .... (8)
9. What .... having a game of tennis? (5)
10. When Paul saw the advertisement, he telephoned Rod .... (11)
15. I'm ill. I'm going to stay in .... (3)
17. What do you like doing in your .... time? (5)
18. You can see films here. (6)
19. Is there a bank .... here? (4)
20. .... don't we go out for a meal? (3)
22. .... as a big supermarket, there are a lot of small shops. (2,4)
25. At the end of the road, turn .... (4)
26. 'How's your stomach today?' 'Not .... good, I'm afraid.' (3)
28. Jack Cooper is the production .... at Western Aeronautics. (7)
29. Turn right at the .... lights. (7)
32. I .... badly, because Mrs Grey snored all night. (5)
33. There's a chemist half way .... Elm Street. (4)
34. She's a .... She works in a hospital. (5)

Down

1. Footballs are .... of leather. (4)
2. What's the shape of this crossword? It's .... (6)
3. Spring, summer, ..., winter. (6)
4. Big. (5)
5. Are there any .... s facilities? Yes, there's a football ground. (5)
6. What's a car made of? .... (5)
7. '.......... .... use your phone?' 'Certainly.' (3,1)
11. Did you .... exercises this morning? (2,3)
12. How many bedrooms .... there? (3)
13. .... for the Rajah, there aren't any good restaurants in Sutton. (6)
14. Hi! My name's Phil. What's .... ? (5)
15. 'Turn round children. I don't want to see your ....' (5)
16. What do people do in discos? They .... (5)
17. I .... a great film yesterday. (3)
21. I want a job .... I haven't got any money. (7)
23. It's hot in here. Can I open a .... ? (6)
24. Not heavy. (5)
26. 'Where did you .... as an engineer, Rod?' 'At an engineering college.' (5)
27. I don't like helping rude passengers. On the .... hand — (5)
28. — I don't .... helping polite passengers. (4)
30. I don't .... very well today. (4)
31. Joan lives in the country, but Sylvia lives in a big .... (4)

Unit 7

What have you got?

Read the conversation between Paul and Jenny. Write more conversations like it, using the pictures.

PAUL: What have you got to read?
JENNY: I've got lots of Agatha Christie books.
PAUL: What else?
JENNY: I've got some magazines.
PAUL: Have you got any newspapers?
JENNY: No, I'm afraid I haven't.

PAUL: ....
JENNY: ....
PAUL: ....
JENNY: ....
PAUL: ....
JENNY: ....

PAUL: ....
JENNY: ....
PAUL: ....
JENNY: ....
PAUL: ....
JENNY: ....

Now write about Jenny, like this:

1. Jenny's got lots of Agatha Christie books and some magazines but she hasn't got any newspapers.

2. ....
....

3. ....
....

_____ Unit 7

In the kitchen

Write down the things you can see in the fridge and in the cupboard. Use There's a/some **and** There are some. **Then say where they are.**

1. There's some milk. .... Where? In the fridge, on the bottom shelf.
2. There are some saucepans. .... Where? In the cupboard, on the top shelf.
3. *There's a chicken.* .... Where? ....
4. .... Where? ....
5. .... Where? ....
6. .... Where? ....
7. .... Where? ....
8. .... Where? ....
9. .... Where? ....
10. .... Where? ....
11. .... Where? ....
12. .... Where? ....
13. .... Where? ....

Now ask someone to get you three things from the fridge, and three from the cupboard.

1. *Could you get me the milk from the fridge?* ....
2. ....
3. ....
4. .... *a saucepan from the cupboard?* ....
5. ....
6. ....

19

Unit 7

Instructions

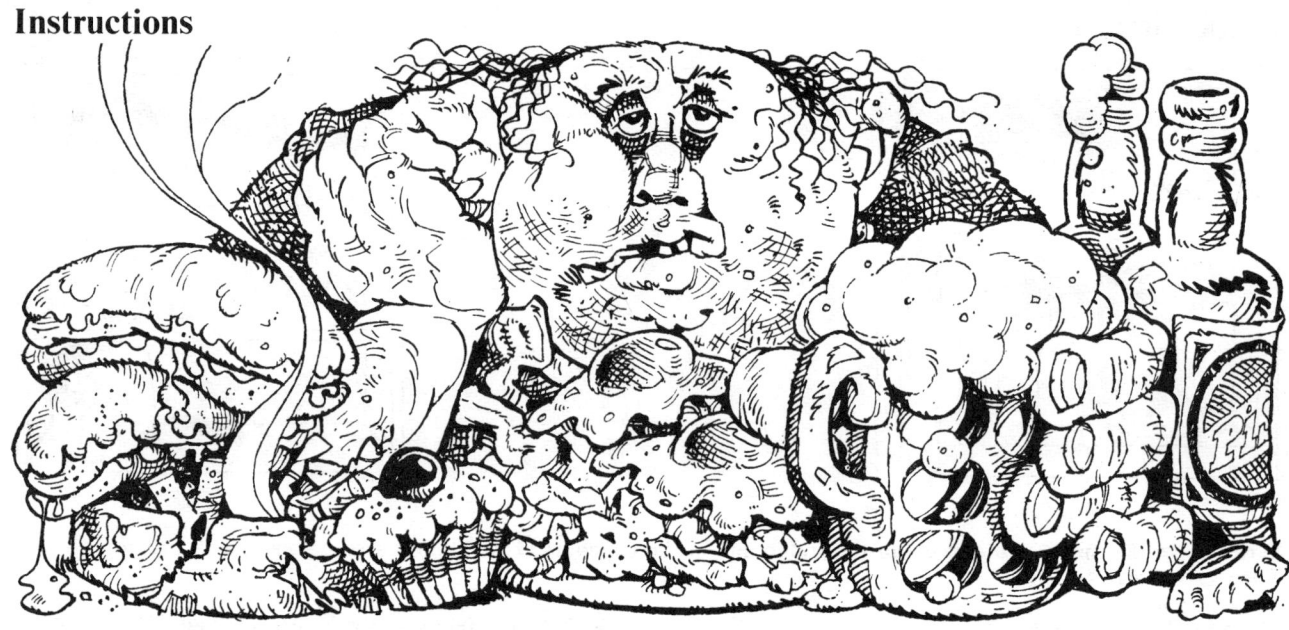

Alec Slugg smokes 40 cigarettes a day. He gets up late every morning, and drives to a café in the next street. He has a big breakfast, and takes 3 spoons of sugar in his tea. Then he drives to the pub, and has 3 or 4 pints of beer, before a big lunch. He never has any fruit after his lunch, because he prefers to have cake or sweets. The only exercise he gets is when he walks upstairs for his afternoon sleep. Later, he has a few more pints of beer, and a big dinner, and then he watches television till midnight. At 2.00 he goes to bed, and has a few last cigarettes, and goes to sleep with all his windows closed.

This morning his car broke down. When he tried to push it to a garage, he suddenly felt very ill. He's going to see his doctor this afternoon.

Write down the instructions you think the doctor is going to give him.

1. Don't drive to the Café – walk instead.
2. Get up early in the morning.
3. ....
4. ....
5. ....
6. ....
7. ....
8. ....
9. ....
10. ....

Vocabulary

Look at the list and write down which things you can buy in these shops: a greengrocer's, a chemist's, a baker's **and** a newsagent's.

| apples | bananas | cabbage | ice cream | matches | potatoes |
| aspirins | bread | cake | magazines | newspapers | shampoo |

Unit 8

Good and bad times to phone

Below are some things that Alice does in the evening.

Which are bad times to phone her? (Write BAD)
Which times are all right to phone her? (Write OK)

She cooks the dinner.	BAD	She does a crossword.	....
She listens to the radio.	OK	She has a shower.	....
She puts the children to bed.	....	She watches her favourite TV programme.	....
She reads a magazine.	....	She chats to her husband.	....

Now write about Alice, like this:

1. *It's a bad time to phone Alice when she's cooking the dinner.*
2. *Alice doesn't mind people phoning when she's listening to the radio.*
3. ....
4. ....
5. ....
6. ....
7. ....
8. ....

Making excuses

A friend telephones Maria and invites her out. Maria has other plans, and refuses. Write their conversations. Choose between I've got to **or** I have to, I'd like to **and** I ought to.

FRIEND: *Would you like to go out for a meal?* (meal?)
MARIA: *Thanks, I'd love to, but I'm afraid I've got to do some work.* (work)

FRIEND: .... (disco?)
MARIA: ....
.... (have a quiet evening)

Unit 8

FRIEND: .... (*party?*)

MARIA: ....

.... (*late night film on TV*)

FRIEND: .... (*play cards?*)

MARIA: ....

.... (*wash my hair*)

FRIEND: .... (*theatre?*)

MARIA: ....

.... (*look after the children*)

FRIEND: .... (*chat?*)

MARIA: .... (*evening class*)

A telephone conversation

David phones Maria one night. Write their conversation in the right order.

MARIA: .... a. I'd love to David, but I'd like to wash my hair tonight.

DAVID: .... b. Sorry, David, but I'm afraid I'm expecting an important phone call later.

MARIA: .... c. Fine. Are you busy? I hope I'm not disturbing you.

DAVID: .... d. Yes. Perhaps I'll be free next weekend.

MARIA: .... e. I'll be quick, then. Would you like to come out to a party this evening?

DAVID: .... f. Fine. I'll give you a ring on Wednesday or Thursday. Bye.

MARIA: .... g. Well, actually, I'm in the middle of painting the garage.

DAVID: .... h. 46791. Maria Carpenter speaking.

MARIA: .... i. OK. Some other time perhaps?

DAVID: .... j. Oh. Hello, David. How are you?

MARIA: .... k. Well, we can go when your hair's dry.

DAVID: .... l. Hello, Maria. This is David.

Unit 8

Comprehension

Read this letter, and then answer the questions below.

> Dear Janet,
> Thanks very much for your invitation to come down to Torquay for the weekend. I'd love to come, but unfortunately August is a bad time for me to get away. We're very busy with the tourists here. At the moment, I'm waiting for a group of Japanese tourists to arrive – I'm actually writing this letter at Heathrow Airport! When they arrive, I've got to take them to their hotel, and then on Saturday I've got to take them on a coach tour of London. I'm free on Sunday, but I really ought to do some housework then. So I'm afraid I can't make it down to Torquay – not until October, anyway.
> Wouldn't you like to come up to London for a day or two instead? I'd love to see you. You can come on a coach tour and help me with the tourists! What about next Saturday?
> Love, Wendy

1. Where did Janet invite Wendy? ....
2. Does she accept the invitation? ....
3. Why is August a bad time for Wendy to get away? ....
4. Is she busy in September too? ....
5. Why is Wendy at Heathrow? ....
6. Where does Wendy invite Janet? ....

Writing

You're an English teacher in London. It's July, and you have a lot of foreign students. On Saturday you're taking a group of students to Cambridge for the day, and on Sunday you're planning to visit your parents, and prepare your lessons for next week. A friend of yours, Eric, has invited you down to the seaside for the weekend.

Write a letter refusing Eric's invitation and explaining why, and invite him up to London.

> Dear Eric,
> Thanks very much .... I'd love .... ,
> but unfortunately ....
> ....
> ....
> ....
> Yours,

Unit 9

Future plans

It's 4.30 on a Friday afternoon. Alma is at work, thinking about her plans for the weekend. Write down the things that she's going to do.

5.00 Go shopping. *In half an hour, I'm going to go shopping.*
5.30 Catch the bus home. ....
6.00 Change clothes. ....
6.30 Leave home. ....
7.00 Collect Bob. ....
7.30 Arrive at the party. ....

Before

It's now 8.00. Write three sentences about Alma, using *before* to link each pair of sentences.

1. *Before Alma* ....
2. ....
3. ....

Asking about holidays

Your friend is going away on holiday. Ask him some questions about it.

YOU: .... ?
FRIEND: To Yugoslavia.

YOU: .... ?
FRIEND: Tomorrow morning, actually.

YOU: .... ?
FRIEND: Oh, for about 2 weeks.

YOU: .... ?
FRIEND: We're driving down there.

YOU: .... ?
FRIEND: In a small guest house in Dubrovnik, on the coast.

YOU: .... ?
FRIEND: Oh, just swim and lie in the sun and relax.

Unit 9

YOU: .... ?

FRIEND: Sorry. The car's full up!

The weather

Write eight sensible sentences from the table.

It's a	good bad	time to	sunbathe go sailing go skiing stay indoors drive	when it's	foggy. snowing. sunny. cloudy. raining. windy.

1. *It's a bad time to sunbathe when it's cloudy.*
2. ....
3. ....
4. ....
5. ....
6. ....
7. ....
8. ....

Reminding people to do things

A friend of yours is going to fly to London tomorrow. Remind him to:

1. visit the Tower of London. 3. visit Madame Tussaud's. 5. send you a postcard.
2. take some photos of London buses. 4. phone your Aunt Juliana in London. 6. bring back some Scotch whisky.

1. *You will remember to visit the Tower of London, won't you?* Yes, I will. Don't worry.
2. *You won't forget to take some photos of London buses, will you?* No, I won't. Don't worry.
3. ....
   .... No, I won't. Don't worry.
4. ....
   .... Yes, I will. Don't worry.
5. ....
   .... Yes, I will. Don't worry.
6. ....
   .... No, I won't. Don't worry.

Unit 9

Comprehension

Read this advertisement for Suntrip Holidays, and answer the questions below.

1. What problems did the Gordons have with
a. travelling?

(i) ....

(ii) ....

(iii) ....

b. accommodation?

(i) ....

(ii) ....

c. the weather?

....

2. On a Suntrip holiday,
a. how do you get there?

....

b. where do you stay?

....

c. who does the housework?

....

d. what about local transport?

....

e. what about the weather?

....

3. What do you have to do on a Suntrip holiday?

....

4. **Write five bad things that aren't going to happen to the Gordons this year.**

(i) *They aren't going to queue for hours for a boat.*

(ii) ....

....

(iii) ....

....

Last year the Gordons went abroad for their summer holiday — by car.

They queued for hours for their boat.
They drove a right-hand drive car in a left-hand drive country.
Their car broke down.
The hotel was uncomfortable.
The food and drink was expensive.
And it rained.

The Gordons are going abroad this summer, too.
But this year, they're going on a **Suntrip Villa Holiday.**

With Suntrip, you fly.
You have your own villa.
You get your own left-hand drive car.
One of our maids cooks, cleans and shops for you.
All you have to do is enjoy yourself.

And we choose our countries carefully — in Suntrip countries it doesn't rain in summer.

The Gordons are going to have a great time.

Before you plan your holiday this year, remember the Gordons, and ask your travel agent about **Suntrip Villa Holidays!!**

We even guarantee the weather!

Unit 9

    (iv) ....
    (v) ....

5. Write five good things that are going to happen to the Gordons this year.

    (i) *They're going to fly.*
    (ii) ....
    (iii) ....
    (iv) ....
    (v) ....

Vocabulary

Write a sentence about the weather in each of these four places.

		C	F	
Bermuda	S	24	75	...
Cardiff	C	13	55	...
London	R	11	52	...
Tunis	F	21	70	...

C – cloud, F – fair, R – rain, S – sun

Unit 10

Talking about people's present lives

Mrs Roberts is very proud of her four children. Look at the information below, and write about their present lives, and what they're hoping to do in the future.

 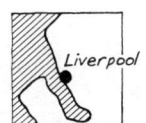   

Jack

Jack Roberts is living in Liverpool, where he's an editor in a publishing company. At the moment, he's studying business in the evenings at Liverpool Polytechnic, and he's hoping to start his own publishing company one day.

Unit 10

Ellen

Ellen Roberts .... where she's a student of .... at .... At the moment, she's producing Hamlet for ....

Fred

....
....
....

Alice

....
....
....

Checking facts about people

A friend is asking Mrs Roberts about her children, but sometimes gets things wrong. Look at Mrs Roberts' answers, and write the friend's questions.

FRIEND: *Jack's living in Southampton, isn't he?*

MRS R: No, not Southampton. Liverpool.

FRIEND: ....

MRS R: No, not London. Cambridge.

FRIEND: ....

MRS R: No, not a boutique. He's working for a publishing company.

FRIEND: ....

MRS R: Yes, that's right. 'Hamlet'.

FRIEND: ....

MRS R: Yes, they're both studying in the evenings.

Unit 10

FRIEND: ....

MRS R: No, not French. English Literature.

FRIEND: ....

MRS R: Yes, that's right. Round the world.

FRIEND: ....

MRS R: No, not an editor. A sailing school director.

FRIEND: ....

MRS R: Yes, I am. Very proud!

Parting remarks

Match the parting remarks in column A with the responses in column B.

A
1. Bye. See you soon.
2. Goodbye. It was nice meeting you.
3. Don't forget to write
4. I must rush, I'm afraid.
5. Have a good weekend.
6. Be good!

B
a. Thanks. And to you.
b. Yes, I'm in a bit of a hurry too.
c. Yes, I will.
d. Yes, I hope we meet again. Goodbye.
e. No. Don't worry. I won't.
f. Yes, I hope so. Bye.

Write your answers here 1 .... 2 .... 3 .... 4 .... 5 .... 6 ....

A conversation

Alice meets an old friend, Martin, in a London street. Write Alice's part of the conversation.

ALICE: *Martin! Fancy seeing you here! How are you?*

MARTIN: Hello, Alice. I'm fine. What about you?

ALICE: ....

MARTIN: I'm working for a chemical company.

ALICE: ....

MARTIN: No, I've left Manchester now. I'm living here in London.

ALICE: ....

MARTIN: She's fine. And so are the kids. What are you doing these days?

ALICE: ....

MARTIN: Oh, are you? That sounds like a good job.

ALICE: ....

MARTIN: French? Why?

29

Unit 10

ALICE: ....

MARTIN: Well, good luck. How are Jack and Fred? And little Ellen?

ALICE: ....

MARTIN: Is she really? Well, give them my regards.

ALICE: ....

MARTIN: Yes, I'm in a bit of a hurry too.

ALICE: ....

MARTIN: Yes, it was nice to see you too. Bye.

Comprehension

The Gordons are having their Suntrip holiday. Read this postcard that Pete Gordon is writing to some friends in England, and answer the questions.

> Greetings from the Mediterranean. Having a great time here – it's really sunny and we're swimming a lot. John's learning to water ski and Katie's visiting all the archaeological sites in the Suntrip car. I'm having a bit of trouble with the left-hand drive but Katie's managing it beautifully. Janet and I are getting a terrific suntan, and I'm taking lots of photographs. The maid isn't very good – she's a student, and she's only working at the villa for her summer holidays. So we're spending a lot of money in restaurants! At least I'm practising my Greek.
> I ran into George Waite yesterday. He's living out here now, and writing novels. He's published two already, and they're doing very well. I'm reading one now, and it's very good. Well – time for a swim. See you soon.
> love Pete.

> Mr & Mrs D. Salter,
> 3, The Dale,
> Petersfield,
> Hants,
> ENGLAND

1. Where are the Gordons? ....
2. Are they enjoying themselves? ....
3. What does Pete say about:

    a. swimming? ....

    b. water skiing? ....

    c. the archaeological sites? ....

_____ Unit 10

d. his suntan? ....
e. his driving? ....
f. photographs? ....
g. restaurants? ....
h. his Greek? ....

4. Write three things about the maid.

   (i) .... (iii) ....
   (ii) ....

5. Write two things about George Waite.

   (i) .... (ii) ....

6. Write three things about his books.

   (i) .... (iii) ....
   (ii) ....

Vocabulary

Look at the list and write down where these people work.

| actress | engineer | nurse | secretary | teacher |
| doctor | librarian | postman | student | waiter |

Unit 11

Crossword

Write the missing words in the crossword.

Clues

Across

1. Drive carefully. It's very .... tonight. (5)

4. I'd love to come, but I'm .... I've got a bad cold. (6)

8. Have we got any .... to eat? (5)

9. To .... you the truth, I'm not feeling very well today. (4)

10. Could you ring back later? I'm .... a shower. (6)

Unit 11

12. John works on an oil .... in the North Sea. (3)
13. Not far. (4)
15. You're an engineer, ...'... you? (5)
18. The saucepans are on the .... shelf. (6)
21. You see with your ....s (3)
23. .... you like to come to the cinema? (5)
24. The ....'.. lovely today. It's very warm and sunny. (8)
25. I've got ..... fish, but I haven't got any meat. (4)
26. 'How .... are you going to stay?' 'About two weeks.' (4)
29. Next to. (6)
31. '.......... you around.' 'Yes, I hope so. Bye.' (3)
33. 'They're in the cupboard.' 'Which cupboard?' 'The small ....' (3)
35. Not dark. (5)
36. 'Give my .... to your wife.' 'Yes, I will. Goodbye.' (7)
37. 'There's a new play at the .... Do you want to come and see it?' (7)
38. 'Sorry, I'm busy.' 'OK. Some .... time, then.' (5)

Down

1. What are Barbara's .... plans? She's going to open branches in other cities. (6)
2. Where are you .... go for your holiday this year? (5,2)
3. This food's made of milk. (7)
4. The top shelf is .... the middle shelf. (5)
5. Look at all those clouds. It's going to .... (4)
6. Rod works in Bristol, ...'...... he? (6)
7. They're staying in a rented .... in Greece. (5)
11. Black + white = ... (4)
14. Paul's got to .... a book about naval engineering. (4)
16. 'You will .... lock the door, won't you?' 'Yes, don't worry. I will.' (8,2)
17. You can buy a paper at a .... agent's. (4)
18. .... Barbara went to Italy, she talked to Gerry. (6)
19. Do you want a bath? There's a clean .... in the bathroom for you. (5)
20. Rod .... Barbara at the Coopers' house. (3)
22. Terry's a carpenter in a small ....ing firm. (5)
27. I'd love to come, but I really .... to have an early night. (5)
28. Sorry I can't see you tonight. I've .... to do some work. (3)
30. 'What's the matter? A headache, I suppose?' 'Yes, ... got a very bad headache.' (1,4)
31. You won't forget to .... the door and lock it, will you? (4)
32. 'I've got some eggs.' 'What .... is there?' 'Only some bread and jam.' (4)
34. Glasgow's in Scotland, ...'... it? (4)

Unit 12

Apologies and explanations

Yesterday, Wendy had to (1) get to school by 8.30 (2) buy a present for her father (3) write to a friend (4) do her maths homework (5) practise the piano. But she didn't do any of these things.

Choose the best explanation for each of the things she didn't do.

a. She lost her purse.
b. Her mother had a headache.
c. She overslept.
d. She lost the address.
e. She left her book at school.

How does Wendy apologise and explain to:

1. her teacher? *I'm sorry I was late for school, but I overslept.*
2. her father? *I'm sorry I didn't*
3. her friend? ....
4. her maths teacher? ....
5. her music teacher? ....

Comparisons

Look at the information below, and make comparisons. Use the adjectives from the list, like this:

long	cold	large
expensive	tall	young
hot		

1. Stephen: 1.80 metres   Margaret: 1.60 metres
   Stephen's taller than Margaret.

2. Belgrade: −10°C   Sarajevo: −15°C
   Sarajevo

3. Stephen: 18 years old   Margaret: 23 years old
   ....

4. Australia: 3 million square miles   USA: 3½ million square miles
   ....

5. River Nile: 6,650 km   River Amazon: 6,400 km
   ....

Unit 12

6. Potatoes: 20p a kilo   Tomatoes: 60p a kilo

   ....

7. Barcelona: 19°C   Beirut: 25°C

   ....

Now rewrite these sentences using adjectives that mean the opposite.

1. England is smaller than France. France *is bigger than England.*
2. Villages are quieter than towns. Towns *are* ....
3. Concerts are duller than discos. Discos ....
4. Bicycles are slower than cars. Cars ....
5. Villages are cleaner than cities. Cities ....

Experiences and impressions

Read the conversation between Jane and Paul, and write similar conversations, like this:

1. Yugoslavia?   JANE: *Have you ever been to Yugoslavia?*
   last year   PAUL: *Yes, I have. I went there last year, actually.*
   enjoy?   JANE: *Did you enjoy it?*
   marvellous!   PAUL: *Yes, I thought it was marvellous!*

2. Stockholm?   JANE: *Have you ever* ....
   last August   PAUL: ....
   like?   JANE: ....
   beautiful!   PAUL: ....

3. horseriding? JANE: *Have you ever done any* ....
   last spring   PAUL: ....
   get on?   JANE: *How* ....
   difficult!   PAUL: ....

4. hitchhiking? JANE: ....
   in June   PAUL: ....
   enjoy?   JANE: ....
   depressing!   PAUL: ....

_____ Unit 12

5. English beer?   JANE: *Have you ever tried*
   last summer   PAUL: ....
   like?   JANE: ....
   delicious!   PAUL: ....

6. steak tartare? JANE: ....
   on Saturday   PAUL: ....
   think of it?   JANE: *What*
   horrible!   PAUL: ....

Linking sentences using Before/After . . . .ing

John is in prison for robbing a bank. Read about what happened, then link the pairs of sentences using After . . . .ing, like this:

1. First John put his gun in his pocket. Then he drove to the bank.
   After putting his gun in his pocket, John drove to the bank.

2. First he put a scarf over his face. Then he went into the bank.
   ....

3. First he pulled out his gun. Then he demanded the money.
   ....

4. First he took the scarf off his face. Then he drove away in his van.
   ....

Now link them using Before . . . .ing, like this:

1. *Before driving to the bank, John put his gun in his pocket.*
2. ....
3. ....
4. ....

Linking sentences using While . . . . was . . . .ing

Unfortunately for John, some things went wrong with his plan. Link the sentences using While . . . . . . was . . . . . . ing, like this:

1. John told the people to put their hands up. At the same time, a secretary quietly went into the back office.
   While John was telling the people to put their hands up, a secretary quietly went into the back office.

Unit 12

2. John put the money into his bag. The secretary phoned the police.

   ....

3. John drove off. A customer wrote down the number of his van.

   ....

4. John drove out of the city. The police stopped him.

   ....

Comprehension

Read the following passage, and answer the questions below.

After drying her hair, Emily got dressed. She looked at her watch. It was 10.00. It was time to go to the hospital. 'Oh dear,' she thought. 'I'm more nervous than I expected.' Before leaving the house, she had a quick look in the mirror, and then she got into her car. While she was driving to the big, grey hospital, she had a last cigarette. Then she arrived. After parking her car, she went in to reception.
  'Dr Meadows, please,' she said.
While she was sitting in the waiting room, she looked at the other people. There were five of them, and they all looked more nervous than she did. After 20 minutes, she heard her name. She stood up and went into Dr Meadows' room. Dr Meadows was about 10 years older than Emily. He smiled. After telling her to sit down, he found her name on his list. Then he looked up.
  'Now, Miss Riley,' he said. 'Have you ever done this sort of work before?'

1. What time did Emily leave the house? ....
2. Where did she have to go? ....
3. How was she feeling? ....
4. What did she do while she was driving? ....
5. What did she do at reception? ....
6. What did she do while she was waiting? ....
7. How did the other people look? ....
8. How old was Dr Meadows? ....
9. Why did Emily go to the hospital? ....
10. Complete these sentences:

    a. Before getting dressed, ...

    b. After looking in the mirror, ...

    c. Before going to reception, ...

    d. Before finding her name on his list, ...

Vocabulary

Write the opposites of these words.

| big | dull | good | long | slow | ugly |
| clean | expensive | hot | narrow | thin | warm |

36

Unit 13

UNIT 13

Asking about and narrating past actions

Police Constable Smith was watching a foreign agent called Zed this morning. Zed was staying at a London hotel. Here are PC Smith's notes:

> 24th Oct. Park Lane Hotel
> Zed
> Breakfast at 8.00 – wearing white suit and dark glasses. Used telephone at 8.30. Went up to room.
> 9.00 came down + luggage. Paid bill, left. Bus → Euston Station. Put luggage down, went into station bookshop.
> Didn't come out. I went in – not there! Opened cases – full of old newspapers. Haven't seen him since!

Inspector Bluff is interviewing PC Smith about what happened this morning.

Fill in the blanks in their conversation.

BLUFF: What time ....?

SMITH: He had breakfast ...., sir.

BLUFF: ....?

SMITH: He was wearing ....

BLUFF: OK. What happened after breakfast?

SMITH: Well, at 8.30, he ...., and then he ....
I waited at reception. At 9.00, Zed .... with his luggage.
After paying ....

BLUFF: Where ....?

SMITH: He .... I followed him.

BLUFF: What .... at the station?

SMITH: Well, sir, he .... and went I
waited outside. He didn't .... so after 10 minutes I
went in too. But he ....!

BLUFF: Did you .... cases?

SMITH: Yes, sir, but ....

BLUFF: Newspapers? I see. Have you seen him since?

SMITH: No, sir, I'm afraid .... I – I've lost him.

37

Unit 13

Clothes and hair

Write the names of the eight pieces of clothing. You'll find the name of another piece of clothing too.

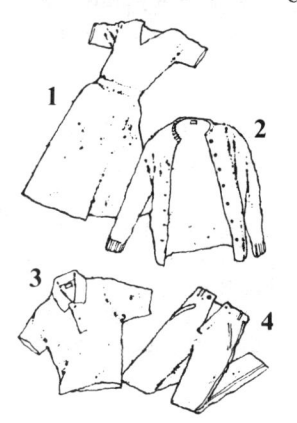

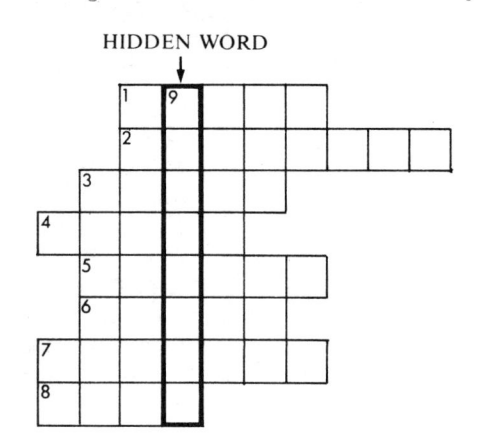

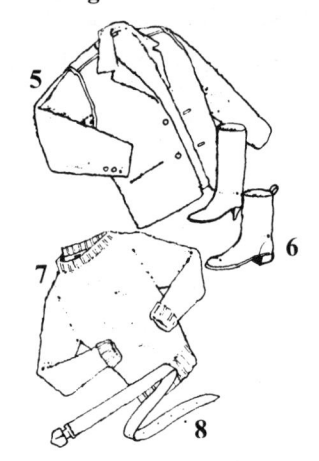

HIDDEN WORD

Now look at the pictures of the boy and the girl, and put the nine words in the spaces below. You'll have to use one word twice.

She's wearing a .... over a checked ....

and a pair of .... She's holding a ....

He's wearing a .... over a striped ....

He's also wearing ...., with a big ....,

and some black ...., and he's holding a ....

Now talk about their hair.

He's got .... hair, and she's got .... hair, with a ....

Now describe these two people.

He's wearing ....

....

She's wearing ....

....

Completed actions

You're having a party tonight. You've made a list of all the things you have to do. When you've done them, you tick them off. Look at the list on the next page:

A friend phones to see how you're getting on. Write parts of your conversation, like this:

1. FRIEND: *Have you taken up the carpet?*
   YOU: *Yes, I've just taken it up.*

Unit 13

2. FRIEND: Have you bought the beer?
   YOU: Not yet. I'm just going to buy it.

3. FRIEND: ....
   YOU: ....

4. FRIEND: ....
   YOU: ....

5. FRIEND: ....
   YOU: ....

6. FRIEND: ....
   YOU: ....

7. FRIEND: ....
   YOU: ....

8. FRIEND: ....
   YOU: ....

List:
1. take up the carpet ✓
2. buy beer
3. prepare the food ✓
4. have a shower
5. change
6. choose the records ✓
7. tell the neighbours ✓
8. set the table

Now you're the friend. Report your conversation in three sentences, like this:

1. He's already taken up the carpet, but he hasn't bought the beer.
2. ....
3. ....
4. ....

Comprehension

Read this news announcement, and answer the questions below.

Police are still looking for the foreign agent Zed. Zed disappeared at Euston Station yesterday morning while police were following him. He was wearing a white suit and sunglasses at the time. Then at 2.00 pm, a policeman saw Zed near the Houses of Parliament. He was wearing a grey raincoat and black trousers, and he was carrying a small bag. The policeman ran after him but Zed jumped into a taxi and disappeared again. An hour later, the police found the taxi at Heathrow Airport. It was empty. The police have received a lot of phone calls today from people in different parts of the country. All of them say that they have seen Zed. 'We've checked most of the reports,' a police officer said this afternoon, 'but we haven't had any luck yet. We think that Zed has left the country, but we're still looking.'

1. Have the police found Zed? ....

2. What was happening when Zed disappeared? ....

Unit 13

3. What was he wearing? ....
4. Where did a policeman see Zed at 2.00pm? ....
5. What was he carrying? ....
6. How did Zed escape from the policeman? ....
7. Where did the police find the taxi? ....
8. What have the police done about the reports? ....

Vocabulary

Answer these questions about clothes.

What do you wear if it's raining? ....

What do you wear if it's snowing? ....

What do you wear if it's sunny? ....

Unit 14

Past events

Mike spent most of this year touring Europe. Here are some of the things he did:

[FEBRUARY] [MARCH] [APRIL] [MAY] [JUNE] [JULY]

It's now December, and Mike's friend Alma is talking to him about his trip. Look at the pictures and answer her questions.

1. ALMA: When were you in London, Mike?

   MIKE: *I was in London about 6 months ago, in June.*

2. ALMA: When did you visit Athens?

   MIKE: ....

3. ALMA: When did you go up the Eiffel Tower?

   MIKE: ....

Unit 14

4. ALMA: When did you see Amy and Jack?

   MIKE: ....

5. ALMA: When did you go skiing?

   MIKE: ....

6. ALMA: When did you break your leg?

   MIKE: ....

How long?

Here's some information about Renée. Ask questions about her, with How long?

1. (going to school: 1965–76) *How long did Renée go to school for?*
2. (living in London: 1976–now) *How long has Renée been living in London?*
3. (London University: 1977–80) ....
4. (working in bookshop: 1976–77) ....
5. (working as chemist: 1980–now) ....
6. (sharing flat with Julia: 1978–now) ....
7. (living on her own: 1976–78) ....

Now answer the questions. Use since **where you can.**

1. *Renée went to school for 11 years.*
2. *Renée has been living in London since 1976.*
3. ....
4. ....
5. ....
6. ....
7. ....

For and since

It's 1984. Alan is telling you some things about himself. Respond like this using for **and** since:

1. ALAN: I came to live in London in 1978.

   YOU: *I see. So you've been living in London for 6 years.*

2. ALAN: I learned to drive 4 years ago.

   YOU: *I see. So you've been driving since 1980.*

Unit 14

3. ALAN: I came to live in this flat in 1980.

   YOU: ....

4. ALAN: I started working for ICI 5 years ago.

   YOU: ....

5. ALAN: I started learning German a year ago.

   YOU: ....

Comprehension

Read this letter of application, and then answer the questions below.

> Dear sir/madam,
>
> I would like to apply for a post as English teacher at your Language Institute.
>
> I was born in Manchester on 19th April, 1956, and went to Manchester Grammar School in 1967, where I studied until 1974. After working as an assistant in W.H. Smith's (Manchester) for a year, I studied English Literature at Aston University. While I was at Aston, I joined the Folk Club, and was the secretary of the University Language Circle. I left Aston in 1978, and since then I have been working at the España School of English in Madrid.
>
> I enclose two references.
>
> Yours faithfully,
>
> *Charles Austen*
>
> Charles Austen

1. Fill in information about Charles Austen on this form.

Name: *Charles Austen* .... Nationality: ....

Date of Birth: .... Age last birthday: ....

Place of birth: ....

Secondary school: .... Dates: ....

University: .... Dates: .... Subject: ....

Other university activities: ....

Employment	Place	Work	Dates

_____ Unit 14

2. **Complete these sentences about Charles:**

a. Charles .... in 1956.

b. .... for 7 years.

c. Charles worked .... for ....

d. .... 3 years.

e. Charles has been working .... for ....

Writing

Now look at the information below, and write an application for the same job from Jenny Black.

Name: Jenny Black		Nationality: Australian	
Date of birth: 6/3/55		Place of birth: Sydney, Australia	
Secondary school: St. Agnes Grammar, Sydney		Dates: 1966-73	
University: Melbourne Dates: 75-77		Subject: Modern Languages	
Other university activities: Drama Club; Sec, University Photographic Soc.			
Employment:	Place	Work	Dates
1.	Plaza Hotel, Sydney	Receptionist	73-74
2.	Ritz School of English, Milan	English teacher	1977-now

```
Dear sir/madam,
    I would like ................................................
............................................................
    I was ....................................................
............................................................
............................................................
............................................................
............................................................
............................................................
............................................................
    I enclose two references.
                    Yours faithfully,
                    Jenny Black
                    Jenny Black
```

43

Unit 15

Travel arrangements

Philip Cork is going on a business trip to Madrid. Answer his questions in the form of a letter to Mr Cork from Freda Curtis, the company's personnel officer.

1. How will I get from the office to the airport? When? (*company car, 10.30*)
2. Who will have the tickets? (*driver*)
3. What time will I check in at the airport? (*11.00*)
4. What time does the plane leave? (*12.00*)
5. How long will the flight to Madrid take? (*2 hours*)
6. Will food be served during the flight? (*lunch*)
7. Will there be anyone to meet me at Madrid? (*representative of the company*)
8. How will he know who I am? (*card – Mr Philip Cork*)
9. Where will he take me? (*Espagnol Hotel, city centre*)
10. What about money? Will he give me any? (*Spanish currency*)
11. When will my first meeting be? (*4.30*)
    Where? Who with? (*main office, Mr French*)

Monday, 12th August

Dear Mr Cork,

<u>Madrid – Travel Arrangements</u>

I enclose details of your travel arrangements for your journey to Madrid on Thursday 15th August.

A company car will take you .... The driver ....

.... You will ....

.... 11.00. ...., and the flight ....

The plane .... Lunch ....

....

There .... He will have .... He .... give ....

.... and ....

....

Your first meeting ....

....

I hope you have a pleasant trip.

Yours sincerely,

Freda Curtis

Freda Curtis
Personnel Officer

Unit 15

Predictions

Cathy and Jim always agree with each other. Here are their answers to a questionnaire about the 21st century.
(✓ = Yes; ✗ = No)

Questions	Cathy	Jim
1. Will there be enough to eat?	✓	✓
2. Will people live in space?	✗	✗
3. Will children learn everything from TV?	✗	✗
4. Will America have a woman president?	✓	✓
5. Will Britain have a king or queen?	✓	✓
6. Will people stop work at 40?	✗	✗

Write conversations between Cathy and Jim, like this:

1. Cathy: *I think there'll be enough to eat.*   Jim: *So do I.*
2. Cathy: *I don't think people will live in space.*   Jim: *Nor do I.*
3. Cathy: ....   Jim: ....
4. Cathy: ....   Jim: ....
5. Cathy: ....   Jim: ....
6. Cathy: ....   Jim: ....

Donald disagrees with all of Cathy's answers. How would he respond to what she says?

1. *Well I don't think there will.*
2. *Well I think they will.*
3. ....
4. ....
5. ....
6. ....
7. ....
8. ....

Now write about Cathy and Jim, like this:

1. *Cathy thinks there'll be enough to eat, and so does Jim.*
2. *Cathy doesn't think people will live in space, and nor does Jim.*
3. ....
4. ....
5. ....
6. ....
7. ....
8. ....

Unit 15

Comprehension

Read the story and answer the questions below.

Do you believe in fortune-tellers? I do. I went to see one last summer. She was a little old lady in a room by the sea. I paid my pound, and sat down, and she looked deep into her large crystal ball.

'You will have a long life,' she said, 'and a happy one. Soon you will start a business, and it will be very successful.'

'Business?' I said. 'But I haven't got any money.'

'Ah, but you will have,' she replied. 'You will meet a very rich girl, and in a year you will marry her. Then you'll start your business. You'll live in a big house and you'll have several children. But . . . but what's this?' She stopped.

'What's the matter?' I asked. 'What can you see?'

'Darkness,' she said. She was looking frightened now. 'You – you will do a terrible thing. You will murder someone! Murder!'

She stood up. The crystal ball hit her while she was running to the door.

I had to do it. I want that business. She won't tell anyone now. Nor will I. And no one else knows.

But you'll agree, I think, that she was a good fortune-teller. She said 'You will murder', and now I have murdered. And tomorrow afternoon I'm going to marry a very lovely, and very very rich, girl.

1. When did the writer go to see the fortune-teller? ....
2. How did the fortune-teller tell the future? ....
3. What were her predictions about the writer's:

   a. life? ....

   b. business? ....

   c. marriage? ....

   d. house? ....

   e. children? ....

4. What happened while she was running to the door? ....
5. Why did the writer kill her? ....
6. What's the writer going to do tomorrow? ....
7. Will the police catch him? ....

   Why/Why not? ....

Unit 16

Crossword

Write the missing words in the crossword.

Clues

Across

1. Tom: 1.90m Jack: 1.85m Tom is .... than Jack (6)

5. .... going out, she dried her hair. (6)

8. Mrs Ingrams .... Mandy 20p to buy some flowers. (4)

9. I've been working there 1979. (5)

10. She's been .... in that house for six years. (6)

11. Have you seen any good films ....ly? (6)

14. You can do this on snow and water. (3)

15. I was born in London, but I .... in Bristol. (4,2)

18. Laura joined a group and began to .... money with her songs. (4)

19. London is .... expensive than last year. (4)

20. When they found the ribbon in the canal, the police .... the police station immediately. (9)

23. Laura was born .... far from this theatre, actually. (3)

25. He was ....ing a white suit. (4)

26. She's got long curly .... (4)

29. When the headmaster came in, the children .... up. (5)

32. Bristol's not in Scotland, ...? (2,2)

33. I studied French .... 4 years. (3)

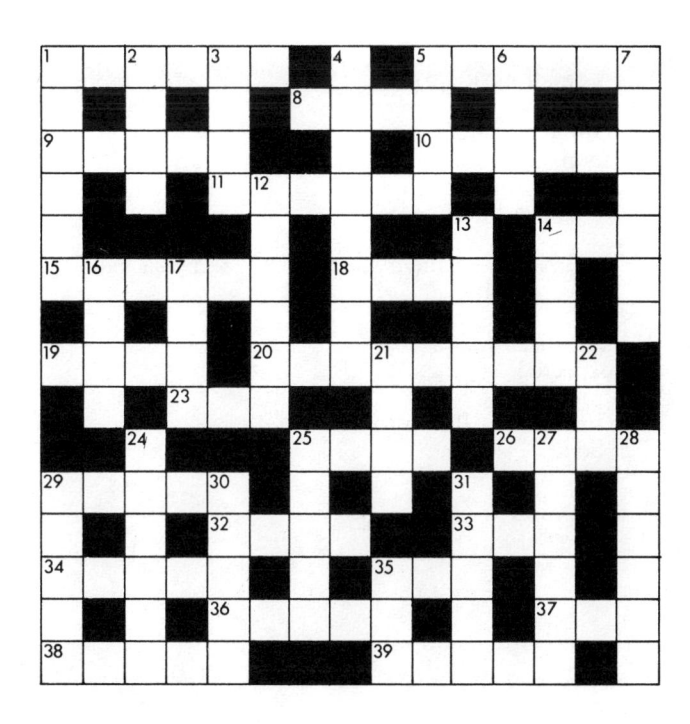

34. Tom's 19, and Jack's 24. Jack is .... than Tom. (5)

35. I haven't .... any money. (3)

36. In 2001, ... will be houses under the sea. (5)

37. I bought this car a long time .... (3)

38. .... I'm late, but I missed the bus. (5)

39. I'm very .... I'm going to bed. (5)

Down

1. And now Laura's going .... her latest song for us. (2,4)

2. How .... did you stay at the party for? (4)

3. 'Have you .... been to Australia?' 'No, never.' (4)

4. They .... studying English since January. (4,4)

5. This holds your trousers up. (4)

6. One year younger than Mandy. (4)

Unit 16

7. You've been learning .... with Building Strategies. (7)

12. Don't worry, Mrs Ingrams. I .... she's just playing truant. (6)

13. A small meal. (5)

14. Don't worry. I'm .... they will come soon. (4)

16. Part of a house. (4)

17. .... the plane took off, Clarissa felt nervous. (4)

21. The disco was livelier .... I expected. (4)

22. 'I think it will rain tomorrow.' 'So ....' (2,1)

24. It's .... in winter than in summer. (6)

25. .... he was waiting, he read his newspaper. (5)

27. The Coopers are going to live .... (6)

28. The police found a piece of .... in the canal. (6)

29. You 25 Across these on your feet. (5)

30. Not clean. (5)

31. .... locking the shop, she went home. (5)

35. What time did you .... up this morning? (3)

LONGMAN GROUP LIMITED,
*Longman House, Burnt Mill, Harlow,
Essex CM20 2JE, England
and Associated Companies throughout the world.*

© Brian Abbs and Ingrid Freebairn 1981, 1984

All rights reserved. No part of this publication may be reproduced, stored in a retrieval system, or transmitted in any form or by any means, electronic, mechanical, photocopying, recording, or otherwise, without the prior permission of the copyright owner.

First published 1981
Sixth Impression 1985
ISBN 0 582 57994 5

Designed by SGS Education, 8 New Row, London WC2 4LH.
Illustrated by Dave Farris and Barry Thorpe.

Printed and bound in Great Britain by
Blantyre Printing and Binding Co. Ltd.